96 HOURS

AN INDIAN'S PLIGHT DURING THE UKRAINAN WAR

SHAYARI BHATTACHARYA

Made with ♥ on the Notion Press Platform
www.notionpress.com

This book is dedicated to the millions of refugees who are displaced from Ukraine and a million others who are unfortunately no-more with us. I would like to add that during the time of devastation and misery, hope and unity is something a person can hold on to. But the backlash from the Indian citizens towards Foreign Medical Graduates was completely out-of-line and cruel. A final dedication to the Indian students whom we cannot see, meet or feel anymore.

Contents

Preface

It is a non-fiction, real account of an Indian as he tries to flee the war waged by Russia against Ukraine. We were in touch with him regularly as he was trying to find a way to leave the country. It was becoming extremely difficult for him with the traffic jams, huge lines at the border, the bombs, the Russian tanks, lack of groceries, and sudden price hikes. We also interviewed some other people of color for their 1st hand experience staying in the war-zone and how they fled or coped with the situation. The main purpose of this book is for everyone to know the real feelings one goes through when survival is at stake.

Acknowledgements

Bezawada Kumar Swamy
Himansh Kumar P
Revanth Raj
Mode Yogananda
Moses Tse Gboga
Dickson Ojama
Gloria Mitongo (Editor)

Prologue

Hi everyone, my name shall not be disclosed for personal reasons, but I wanted the world to know what happens when you stay in a war zone. It is easy for everyone else to send messages and prayers, but this written account will help everybody know the plight of the people, especially foreign students living in Ukraine. There has been a recent trend to disgrace the foreign medical graduates in India, to which I have nothing to say. Hopefully, this story of mine will help clear the conscience.

I am Indian, studying medicine in the westernmost city of Ukraine, Lviv. I originally belong to a southern state called Andhra Pradesh. Lviv is known to be the most peaceful city in Ukraine. I have been here since 2017 and am about to finish the 5th year of my medical studies. It is an option that seemed fit to me, keeping monetary sources and the advantages of being near to Europe similar to 20,000 other Indian students who are also stuck in Ukraine. This is my story, which I want everyone to know.

CHAPTER ONE

The Last Normal Day

23/02/2022 (Wednesday)

Thanks to online classes, I didn't even wake up as we started our class at 11:30 AM. It was epidemiology. The class was super boring. I wish our teacher could take classes at night so that I can have a good night sleep. Also, I should stay awake as she can ask us a question anytime. Something you need to know about our classes in Ukraine. Our lessons consist of lectures and practicals. While nobody cares about the lectures, you need to pass each practical lesson. The marking system is same as the European one. You will be marked out of 5, where 5 is the highest, 3 is the least, and 2 is fail. I never intend to get the highest marks, I just want to pass each class with either a 3 or a 4. That is enough for me. My teacher kept talking and talking. I had my headphones on. With my audio and video off, I went to the bathroom and brushed my teeth. I opened my Instagram and WhatsApp for messages. There were none. I went to the kitchen and made some tea for myself. I stayed in India for almost 6-7 months during the pandemic and got a habit of drinking tea first thing in the morning. Medically speaking, it is not a good habit.

It was about 2 PM when it was my turn to answer her question. I had the book, which I opened only on Wednesdays for each Epidemiology class. But most of the time, you cannot find the right answer in the book. Thanks to Dr. Google, I received a 4 today in my Epidemiology class. The class finished after an hour. I live in an apartment with 2 roommates, Raj and Adi (names changed). I don't interact with them unless it is time for rent or there is some issue with the plumbing or electricity. They belonged to Telangana State, and we all spoke the same language, i.e. Telugu. I unfortunately don't speak a lot of Hindi, but I do understand it.

At about 4 PM, I dragged myself out of the bed to take a shower. I think, the last time, I took a shower was Monday. The cold winters together with the laziness of online classes made "taking a shower" a task. It is like a thing that you need to write down in your to-do list. Before taking the shower, I thought I will glimpse through the news. There have been recent tensions between Ukraine and Russia, with Russian tanks and soldiers lining up near the border. Putin, however, said it is just a military drill, nothing to worry about. If Ukraine joins NATO, then Russia would definitely attack. That was a straight threat to EU and NATO. I wasn't worried much. I thought it will be same as my seniors faced back in 2014. They carried out their day-to-day life like nothing happened. There was a spike in prices and Ukraine's economy crashed. It was not a problem for us as we received our money in dollars, which even gave us an advantage as compared to the Ukrainians.

My parents have been bugging me to come back to India because of the escalating situation. I assured them that it was just a threat and nothing will happen. But then I saw my friends going back to India, and so I booked a cheap flight to India on 7th March. The Indian embassy had asked us to register with them so that they know our names and locations in case they have to evacuate 20,000 Indians. Yes, you heard me right, there are about 20,000 to 30,000 Indian students currently staying in Ukraine. They had arranged flights for Indians which were about 800USD for one way. All they can do is cash in on people's miseries. I wasn't worried a bit. I thought like the maximum Russia will do is maybe try to invade Kyiv (the capital) but definitely nothing will happen to Lviv.

I got so engrossed in the news, that I completely forgot about paying my tuition fee. Today was the last day, otherwise I have to pay a fine for paying the tuition late. The school had released a circular providing us with permission to leave for our respective countries given that we have paid our tuition fees. Since I had already booked my flight, why wait!

The banks in Ukraine stay open till 5 PM or 6 PM depending on the bank, unlike the Indian banks. I did not take the shower as I intended, changed my clothes, wore a jacket and left the apartment with my money and my slip. Paying tuition is a tedious task on a normal day. With the given circumstances, there was a huge line of students. I should have been done by an hour, it took almost 2 hours for the same process. An important step in paying the tuition is submitting the slip from the bank to the administrative office of our university. There have been cases when even after paying the tuition, the university accused students of not paying and if you are clever enough to take a photo of the receipt from the bank, you are saved otherwise you might have to pay again if you have no way to prove you paid. The process was brutal and tiresome. I had created a special file in my phone and a physical file with all my receipts since the past 4 years. In addition to that, since I was in the bank, I decided to withdraw all of my dollars. War or not, all these tensions are definitely showing some economic issues. Before, the bank goes bankrupt, it is better I take my dollars.

In the middle of the tuition-fees-paying chaos, my Iranian senior, Mohammed (name changed) called. He was in town and wanted to meet. I met him when other senior Ashok (name changed) was in Ukraine. Ashok was from Telangana too. He was my first friend in Lviv. He is in India right now practicing medicine. I know all of Ashok Anna's (Anna is basically a Telugu term for elder brother) friends since I used to hang out with him all the time. I miss him terribly. Mohammed Anna, on the other hand, decided to stay in Ukraine. I told him that I was in the middle of paying my fees and will call him back once I am done, and when I reach home. By the time we met, it was almost 5 PM, and he was getting late because he wanted to leave the same day and go back to Kyiv, where he lived now. He got a chicken burger for me from McDonald's. How thoughtful of him!! I have been starving too because all I had from the morning was a cup of tea. He did not come inside, and we exchanged our greeting, then he left. Mohammed is big on talking. He can go on and on about stuff, he has no knowledge or experience in. But this time, he seemed like he is in hurry and left quickly.

Finally, I was free, and I could take that shower. I started the hot water. It usually takes about 5 to 10 minutes for the hot water to finally make its appearance in my flat. It is beyond annoying when you are in a hurry, and then you wait eternally for hot water. Thankfully, there is a bathtub where I can forget all my sorrows for a few fleeting moments. The water was just as much warm as I needed it to be. Just as I was dipping my legs into it, I heard my phone ringing. I thought I will ignore it, but usually it doesn't stop there. Does it? I wrapped a towel around my waist and went out of the bathroom and saw it was my girlfriend. I have been seeing someone since the past 5 years. Shivani (name changed) is an amazing woman. Innocent, honest, and naive. Yes, her naïveté can be annoying sometimes, but I enjoy every moment when she listens to me with her big pretty eyes. So, I am basically pretty much mad about her and would cross an ocean or jump from a mountain for her or whatever it is you want to say. She lives in India and our long-distance relationship is not without any problems. We had our share of issues to be sure, but we overcome them each time. I may have seen her for like 2-3 times since I started dating her. If I ignore her call now, it would be another scandal later on. In addition to that, there is the tense situation created by Russia. I answered her call and went into the water. I knew it is going to be awhile. She was up-to-date about the ticket to India, the Russia-Ukraine tension, and basically my daily schedule. She was delighted that I was coming back to India. We have barely seen each other between my family and friends. You see, not everyone knows about our relationship. Only my best-friend in India, my mother, my sister, and Ashok Anna know. We celebrated maybe 3 birthdays and never celebrated an anniversary since the past 5 years. So, we were making plans in India, what we will do, where we will go, which movies we can watch. The call went on for about 2 hours. One question that everyone raises is whether I have a sex-life or not. Well, let's keep this book family-friendly. Shall we? It should suffice by saying, "Yes, I have an amazing sex-life with my one and only Bangaram." I call her Bangaram, which in Telugu language means gold.

Time flew like it had to catch a flight or something. It was already 7PM. I wanted to study something for tomorrow's test. It was pediatric surgery and our professor's class is basically a set of random questions randomly thrown at us. There was no way to open a website or any book. Apart from that, she does not give you time. It leaves me with no choice but to study. I hated her but, in a way, I was actually putting in real efforts and learning a lot. I opened the book, which was utterly boring. Therefore, I decided to go through a YouTube video about the topic. I was deeply engrossed into the topic intussusception and the surgical complications that might arise, I got a text from Ashok anna asking if I was ready for the English class. Because of the test tomorrow, I said I will join a bit late. After making some notes, 2-3 videos, and skimming through the online medical dictionary, I felt like I was ready for tomorrow. I texted Ashok anna back and we started out English lesson, where he tries to help me with my speaking and writing skills. I wanted to give IELTS exam so that I can write PLAB (medical exam to become a registered practicioner in the United Kingdom). In other words, he was trying to help me express myself better in English. After the lesson, I told him about my ticket to India. He laughed to that saying he knew that would happen. Also, he asked if I would join him to go to Goa. I said "of course, why not. But I would need about 10 days after I reach India." He continued to explain his plan and what he had decided for us. It all seemed very exciting.

Finally, I ended the lesson and I felt my stomach churning with hunger. I went into the kitchen and decided to boil some rice. Furthermore, I think my roommates had already eaten. Rightfully so, it was 12 AM. I was this dysfunctional person, surviving on pickles and rice and sleeping at 2 AM and waking up according to my class. I was one of those people with high metabolism so whatever I eat, I never get fat. Some people think I am so lucky, but truly I was not happy. I wish to be heavier and muscular. I always look for ways to gain weight and become bigger. I have tried some protein powder but due to the addition of steroid, I started avoiding them.

My meal was so satisfying, I thought I cannot walk and my stomach was about to burst. I started scrolling through the social media posts where everyone talked about their version of what Russia might or might not do. I quickly drifted into a deep sleep thinking that it is all just a hoax.

CHAPTER TWO

96 Hours

24/02/2022 (Thursday)

I woke up to the sound of a siren in the morning at about 7 AM. I have been hearing news about some bomb shelling in the DONBAS region as opposed to Kyiv which is what I expected. Although I did not hear any gun-shots or bombarding, there was an aura that I won't be able to describe. My roommates and I weren't sure what to do. We all decided to stay calm and contact the embassy. It was about 9 AM when I wanted to get a coffee when my roommate Raj told me that there is Martial law in Ukraine and that there have been airstrikes all over Ukraine.

The embassy did not provide any official news of evacuation but they said that the process was on the way. I went to the bathroom to carry out my daily morning routine when I was interrupted by an email saying my flight which was scheduled to India on 7th March has been canceled. That was to be expected with the Martial law and closed airspace and the airstrikes. When I heard Ivano-Frankivsk and Kyiv being 2 of the other cities being hit, my heart sank because that meant a full-scale invasion. It also meant I was right which I did not want to be. I immediately tried to contact my friends in Ivano-Frankivsk to which they responded frantically saying the airport has been hit and they have gone down in their bunkers. Although everyone was safe, I could sense intense fear for life in their voices. It was like overnight, everyone's purpose changed. One wanted to excel in his/her lessons, another wanted to impress a girl from class but today everyone just wanted to be able to survive. Within 2-3 hours, things became very clear that Putin was not just trying to threaten Ukraine. He was determined to take over the country at all costs. The embassy advised us to stay calm but I felt like those words did not make sense anymore. The situation was not one to be calm anymore. We needed solutions and ways to get out.

While Kyiv got the biggest hit, I got the news that all the Indians were kept at a secure bomb shelter near the Indian embassy. One of my friends even tried to leave today but the flight got canceled in the early morning hours. No sign or news of evacuation yet. Being in L'viv has its advantages of being near the border to cross Poland. I was still hopeful since a war-like situation occurred in 2014 when Russia took a part of Ukraine in the east called Crimea. We all thought maybe these explosions were a way to create a threatening situation for Ukraine and a message to the EU. Shortly after, there were social media pictures of buildings hit, explosions, and tanks entering from 3 sides of Ukraine. Even Belarus decided to let the Russian army use their territory to attack Ukraine. It was already 5 PM when it was crystal clear that Putin wanted a war. There were reports of huge sanctions which would be soon placed on Russia and diplomacy but had no effect on the Russian President's decision to assault Ukraine. I am not Ukrainian but I was under attack too and all I wanted to do at that point was to leave Ukraine.

I had a long talk with my parents who stay in a small village near Vijayawada, a big city in the state of Andhra Pradesh in India. I thought they would lecture me on how I should have listened and that I am not a good son. It was actually the opposite. They were supportive, strong, and showed empathy towards my situation. My mother tried to hold her tears back but she couldn't. Looking at their support, my internal strength grew and I knew exactly what I have to do. We had to go to the border and cross it somehow. The Indian embassy was taking too long to respond. Taking important decisions in the spur of the moment was not my strongest suit. But the situation demanded otherwise. Februarys are always cold in Ukraine. It was -4-degree Celsius that day but the war and the hatred made it colder. I had long discussions with my 2 roommates for about 2-3 hours. Raj was adamant that we wait for the embassy to arrange something while Adi wasn't sure what to do. Adi just said "I won't be left alone here. If you guys move, I will go with you. I should have studied harder during my MCET days." MCET is an exam in the Telangana state of India to get medicine and engineering seats provided by the Govt. A slight peek as to why every year almost 40,000 to 100,000 students decide to study abroad.

The main reason is the lack of admissions. The number of medicine aspirants ranges from 500,000 to 600,000 while the number of students who will be accepted is merely 10,000. It is not even 1%. I do not want to go into the details about the reservations, bribery, cheating, and fraudulent activities in such exams and during admissions. If you are from a rich family, you might be able to send your child to a private institution that costs anywhere between 5L (approx. 7000$) to 12L (approx. 17,000$) per semester. This excludes the "donations" given by "benefactors" or "charity". I simply responded by saying there is no point pondering and crying over the past. We need to come up with solutions to leave Ukraine as soon as possible. I even spoke to Ashok anna who was currently practicing medicine in India. In conclusion, we decided to try to go to the border the next day since today it was already 8 PM. We planned to take all the important documents, a few undergarments, a pair of clothes, some chips and a bottle of water in our backpack. A major question was how will we reach the border since it was about 70km away from where we were staying currently. With buses, taxis, and all other forms of public transport closed, it was difficult to get from one place to another without your car.

Several audios and pictures flooded the Indian community that they were being denied to cross the border. There was a wait of over 10 hours already. I did not want to be demotivated by those otherwise I will be stuck here forever. Headlines for 24 Feb read that Russia has launched missiles over Ivano-Frankivsk, Kyiv, Kharkiv, Dnipro, Odesa, and Mariupol. No civilians were killed and Russian troops entered Kyiv. It was scary just like it sounded on the news. I was quite worried for my Indian friends in Kharkiv, Odesa, and Kyiv that were heavily hit and were surrounded by troops from everywhere. The EU was still deciding on what to do but one thing was clear Ukraine was alone in this war. Nobody would come and help them. As per the international and local news about 50,000 people have already crossed borders in Poland, Romania, Hungary, and Moldova. The Ukrainian govt. needed more soldiers and therefore issued a rule to let women and children pass the border but not the men from age 18 to 60. But where does that leave us? Are we allowed to cross any border? Which border was easiest and fastest to cross?

My thoughts were broken by a phone call from Mohammed. I thought he would have answers to all my questions since he usually does. Unfortunately, he didn't. He was stuck in a bunker under his flat with his brother and brother's girlfriend. Everybody was fine on his part. He said the bomb landed near his apartment and that he was scared too but he will find a way to get out of Kyiv. For him, that should definitely be the priority as the Russian soldiers close in on the capital. There was curfew during the whole day and night so he said he would probably leave with his brother and others the next day towards L'viv. I reassured him that he can stay here but I knew that nobody wanted to stay in Ukraine anymore. I also said that he should try to stay indoors because of the heavy bombarding and firing. He responded by saying that they aren't even allowed outside. He reassured me that everything is going to be fine and that we will get out of this mess. Mohammed is known for his pessimistic views and worries. This time he showed exceptional courage to save his brother and everyone else he can save including 2 other Iranian and 2 Arabic friends of his apart from his brother.

With all these worries aside, I completely forgot about Shivani who has been calling me since morning. I had texted her that I am safe and that nothing had happened here. But of course, that wasn't enough. I have to say that it wasn't easy with the insecurities but I had faith in her and in our relationship. I also hadn't eaten anything so I decided to make some Ukrainian Maggi as it was almost 10 PM. I saw 5 missed calls from my girlfriend as she was watching the wrong news (Whatsapp news) and texted me about those links saying if I were okay. I texted her saying I will eat and call her in 30 minutes. I also told her that the links, pictures, and videos she was sending were fake and gave her the right news to follow. I also told her to follow Zelensky (President of Ukraine) on Twitter, and the official Indian embassy page on Facebook to get the right updates. Now that I think of it, I might have been a bit harsh with her and sidelined her. I don't know how I would have acted if our positions were reversed. I wanted to have a change of environment so I decided to eat while watching the local Telugu comedy show.

However, I could not shake the fear I felt in my gut. The uncertainty and the long-term consequences of this Russian assault on Ukraine might be disastrous for my university and my studies. I have invested so many years and what if all this goes to waste. That lingering questions never left my subconscience. I tried to put those thoughts away and laugh as the comedians were making vague jokes. It was almost 11 PM in Ukraine when I called my girlfriend back. She picked it up within a ring and started crying. I just let her cry because there was nothing I could do. I wish I could be out of this mess and be with her but unfortunately, I wasn't. I broke the silence after some time with a "How are you?" She was wiping her nose as I figured from the sound saying "what will happen to me!! I am fine. It is you I am worried about." I just replied that "see, worrying will just lead to problems and not solutions. All I need is support and solutions." She agreed to that and asked, "so what is the plan?". We had a 2-hour long conversation where I tried to explain all possible routes to leave in addition to the ones suggested by the Indian government. She seemed comparatively calm and we even joked about our days together in India. They were few but memorable. I told her that I would have to leave for the border early in the morning and I must sleep. She said "yes. Of course. Please keep texting me the updates." After putting the call down, I started packing my bag with my other roommates. I recommended taking just a back-pack to which everyone agreed. My owner showed great support by contacting a taxi driver the next day morning at 6 AM. We were ready. Ready to leave.

CHAPTER THREE

72 Hours

25/02/2022 (Friday)

I didn't have much sleep throughout the night. Who can sleep when you don't know where the next bomb is going to land!! I was talking to my roommates for a long time and we had quite some stories to share. I am not much of a chatter. I like to stay silent and observe but I tend to overshare with friends who are close to me. Those are few. Yes, these are uncertain and tragic times but they also bring you together. I don't remember at what time I slept but I woke up with a sudden "thud" sound. After a bomb blasts, any loud sound scares you. It was just the window that was forced to open by strong winds. It was 4 AM. I decided to clean my room and keep things in their places. The cleanliness around me might help to declutter my mind. It will not help the feeling of helplessness, loneliness, and sadness that I felt. Come to think of it, it might have been a cry for help.

I was lost in cleaning when suddenly my alarm rang. It was 5:30 AM. I went to wake up my roommates who were also up and were getting ready for the day. In my sleeplessness, I also created a list including the most important things which were documents, passport, temporary residency, cash, card, some clothes, food, and water. The aim was to check and tick things off after packing so that we did not miss the most important things. Everything checked out perfectly. 23rd morning was perfect in the sense that the sun was shining brightly and the birds were out chirping. Little did they know that Russia had bigger plans. The bombings were killing thousands of animals and mother nature was suffering.

I recharged my phone to carry out international calls and had internet money too. We started our journey at exactly 6 AM when we sat inside the taxi and he drove us to the border. The traffic was immeasurable. In Ukraine, you do not see such traffic jams as the ones in India. Well, it is understandable since everybody wants to leave and get to safety. As the taxi driver was driving us, the day seemed all normal except that there were fewer people on the streets and more vehicles on the road. Nature gleamed in the sunshine which was a sign of spring coming in soon. This time, it did not bring joy. The trees, the leftover snow, the sun, and the blooming flowers did not make any sense and certainly did not spark happiness as the past years did. All I could think about is crossing the border and getting back home into my mother's arms. She has been worried sick. She tried not to show that. Probably she wasn't able to eat anything the previous night.

It took about 2 hours for us to reach the border when the cab driver stopped and signaled us to leave. I couldn't see any line and we all were momentarily happy. It was rudely interrupted by the cab driver when he said in a Ukrainian accent "You need to walk 5-6km. I not go further". We gave him the money as we promised (50 USD) and left. It was a tough time and everyone was trying to cash in. A usual taxi ride in L'viv used to be 5 USD while the cab driver was now demanding nothing less than 50USD. Anyways, we got down and started our walk in the cold. It was about 8 AM and the walk would take at least 1-2 more hours to reach the security check-post. After getting down, the first thing I asked my roommates was if they had their backpacks, passports, and everything else they brought. "Yes", they said unanimously. I had texted my girlfriend that I will try to cross the border and asked her to send the message across to my parents too. My sister and my mother know about her. It is just my father. He is a strict man with a set of conservative rules that do not fit today's world. I was looking forward to breaking the news to him later this week but then Russia decided to invade a war that was last seen during the 2nd world war. My seniors had warned me about the poor signal reception at the border. I had tried to contact the embassy but nothing. We had finished about a mere kilometer when Adi was like "look there are some Indians. Maybe they have some news". Raj mumbled "well, they are coming back. I don't think it is any good." I was determined to cross the border no matter what anyone says. I did not know them personally but they too studied at the same university as I was. As soon as we reached, they started saying "there is no point. They are misbehaving and pushing us back in line. We need to go with the embassy" without even asking them anything. Adi and Raj agreed to that and said that we must head back. I took them to a side and responded "we came this far. Let us at least know if it is allowed or what is the process or which border we should cross. Maybe they will allow it. That news might not be real." Raj said "I don't know bro. If Indians were allowed to go across the border, they would have crossed. Why would they come back and what will they gain from lying." Adi added "I agree. See I understand you want to cross the border, we all do. But we need to come up with a better plan. Maybe if we are in a bigger group, it would be better. Have you seen what the officials are doing with us?" My heart almost skipped a beat when I saw the video, that Adi showed, wherein two Indian boys were being pushed back, beaten up, and not allowed to cross the border. I was afraid but still, I insisted on walking towards the Ukrainian-Polish border of Rava Rus'ka.

The walk after that discussion was eerily silent. I knew they did not agree with what I said however, I was thankful that they did not leave me alone. Sometimes the best of friendships come alight in the worst of times. The funny thing was that I wasn't even close to my roommates before this situation occurred. I always thought that they are different and somehow resentful because of the differences between Telangana and Andhra Pradesh. Earlier it was one state but later there was a huge protest to separate which finally took place in 2013. I had no hard feelings whatsoever. Turns out neither did they. In fact, anyone who belongs to Telangana or Andhra Pradesh did not contain any resentment except maybe some far-right or far-left extremists. All everybody wants are basic stuff like water, food, shelter, education, and healthcare.

Suddenly I started seeing a commotion and immediately understood that it was the line to cross the border. There was a wave of disappointment when I saw a huge group of Indians standing aside and not in line. I am not an expressive extrovert. My roommates ran towards them with 100 questions randomly being shot at them. I stood at the back listening to their disappointing noes and negations. I tried to see if there were any foreigners in the line but I couldn't figure out anyone. My attention from the line was broken when I heard that 3 Keralites crossed the border from Shehyni district in Ukraine, another border check-post with Poland. I asked how did they pass and if they were stopped or beaten up but nobody has an answer for that. Maybe they were lucky or they had a visa. They contacted their friends shortly after crossing but soon after there was complete silence from those 3 students. They could not be reached out anymore, and nor did they give them more information. I do not understand why Indians like to abandon others. Is it jealousy? Is it a plain non-caring attitude? I will never know. or maybe it is population leading to competition. Hopefully, everyone is not like that. After a 5-6 hour wait, long baseless discussion, I agreed with everyone that we have to go back. I might have been good at hiding what I was feeling but this time it was different. I wanted to cry, shout, and laugh at the same time. "Maybe I am going mad," I thought to myself. "I have to keep it together. The Russian soldiers will certainly not throw me out of my house and execute me. Right? Their fight is against the current government."

A sudden ping on my phone broke my chain of thoughts. It was Ashok anna who was trying to know if I was successful in crossing the border. I just replied with a "No." I felt alone, scared, and extremely cold. It was as if the weather decided to mimic my feelings. We waited for a car that can take us back. Several men left their families off at the border and helped us get back to our places in L'viv. Earlier whenever I used to come back to L'viv, it felt like home. Today it was foreign to me. The helplessness of the people, closed shops, and the cold weather did not make anyone happy. Reaching my home, I threw my bag and coat on the bed and began scrolling on my phone. The situation had worsened with marching Russian troops from every border towards major Ukrainian cities like Kyiv, Kharkiv, and Odessa. The city I stayed in was still a haven where everybody wanted to come. I know I shouldn't complain but who knows what President Putin was going to do. What if the next bomb is on my building?

It was almost 6 PM by the time I freshened up after reaching home. There was no time to dwell upon the disappointment but to come up with a plan. I schemed through everyone's status when one of my Tamilian counterparts said they are arranging a bus. I immediately wrote a message saying, when they will go and where. The Tamilian guy might have taken 5 minutes to answer but it felt like more than an hour. He said the next morning they want to try to cross the border from Shehyni district. There were a total of 30 Tamilians who were in that group. That news was like a ray of sunshine in a really dark tunnel. I asked if they have a place for 3 more people. They replied affirmatively and said "Of course. Meet us tomorrow at 8 AM near the 3rd hostel." The happiness and proudness I felt were beyond explanation.

Adi and Raj were happy too knowing there is something to look forward to. Going by bus with such a huge group might act as an advantage. They might not stop you and check everyone collectively. Or at least that was the hope.

On the other hand, the Iranian senior was on the move too. He left Kyiv at about 8 AM today and was able to cross the city without any issues. When I say issues, I am talking about bombings, deaths, encounters with tanks, or soldiers. Of course, the traffic was above and beyond. It was chaotic. Traffic rules were not being followed and almost every person was out on the streets trying to flee the city. The city is a host to about 28 lakh people. About half of them were on the streets since the morning after the curfew was lifted. I mean, who can blame them. They want to reach safety as do I. There were several more alarming bombings in the city. Usually, it takes about 5-6 hours by car to travel from Kyiv to L'viv but it has been about over 12 hours and he had just come halfway. The traffic was ruthless and expectedly everyone was petrified. I had a small talk with my parents who were just happy to see me alive. I started with the good news that we would try to leave the country tomorrow with 30-40 other Indians. They were like "yes, we heard that from your friend." My father continued "I have complete confidence in you, son. You will find a way. It will be difficult but just don't give up." I was trying to listen to my father but couldn't help but notice that he was trying to hide his tears as well. My mother added, "Son, have you eaten anything?" I lied "yes, I had some food on the way." The sadness and disappointment had completely killed my appetite. I ended the call after about an hour giving them the details of the travels and how the embassy is unresponsive to us. They were busy evacuating the Indians from the east. They started "Operation Ganga" which aimed at evacuating all 20,000 Indian students from Ukraine and sending them back to India for free. I don't know how effective and helpful the operation would be but that was a hope that I would hold on to. At about 10 PM, I thought I should eat something. I made some rice and ate it with a pickle. That was one of the easiest dishes one could eat and my mother's pickles were amazing. I was thrown away by calls and messages at once. My girlfriend knew that I wasn't able to cross the border. I had a long 1 hour- 1 hour 30 minutes call with her. I could hear trembling in her voice but she was trying to stay strong. I said, "right now the city I am in, is the safest and thousands of people from eastern parts have fled from all over." I don't know how helpful the call was for her but it surprisingly increased my strength to look for a way out of the devastating war.

The headlines that day were terrifying as hell. Russian troops had marched right into the heart of the country. There was heavy shelling in Kyiv which meant that Russian troops were bombarding the city's key military areas. Yes, they said that only the military areas were hit but there were incidents when some residential buildings were hit too. None of the Indians were injured or dead yet so that was good news but many Ukrainians (198 to be specific) died. The president declared that they had no support from their so-called allies and that the civilians must join the fight and make homemade bombs. Thousands of residents were in the underground metro station in Kyiv that was safe from the aerial bombarding. A woman even gave birth in one of those underground bunkers. I thought of what the children are going through and how will they come out of this trauma. Many adults and children will probably suffer from PTSD (Post traumatic stress disorder). Basically, they go through psychological turmoil even after the war is over. their lives will never be the same after this.

I felt happy that I was not in Kyiv but the thought of something like that happening in L'viv shook me from the inside out. For now, the important fact was that Ukraine was still under democratic administration and that my city was safe. It was already 2 AM and I hadn't eaten anything. I went to the kitchen to find whatever is left. The fridge was empty. There were some potatoes which I boiled and ate fearing what will I do tomorrow. My happy thought told me "Tomorrow you will be across the border." I decided to stop looking at news and social media because everything was about the Russian invasion. I decided to watch a random movie. My thoughts, however, were about tomorrow and how I might get freedom (emphasis on the word "might)" but the recent events did not leave me with much of a choice but to think negatively.

CHAPTER FOUR

48 HOURS

26/02/2022 (Saturday)

I blamed Russia for the harsh weather we woke up to. There was no glimpse of the sun but my heart was gleaming with hope and faith as today would be the day I might reach safety. Since I slept around 3 AM yesterday, I woke up at 7:30 although my alarm rang like 10 times probably since 7 AM. I dragged myself across the hall to the bathroom and brushed my teeth. While I was looking in the mirror, I told myself that today would be different. Today I will not be worried and I will and I must cross the border. But there was a lurking question of what if I don't make it? What if they don't let us cross the border? What if they pressurize the men (doesn't matter which nationality) to fight? It was a difficult thought to shrug off. Hearing my roommates shouting from his room to get ready, I finished brushing, peed, washed my face, and went out. My bag pack was ready just like yesterday and we were ready just like yesterday.

At 8 AM exact, the three of us were standing in front of Hostel no. 3. But I could not see anybody else. Panicking, I thought "Have they left us"? I took out my phone in the freezing wind and called the guy whom I spoke with yesterday. He sounded like he was still sleeping. I said "I am sorry. It is 8 AM and we are waiting out here in the cold." To that he responded with anger "haven't you heard? The officials are discriminating against us. They haven't let any Indian or foreigner pass through these borders. We canceled the bus." I was like "umm yes, I have heard that but since we are a huge group, they might allow us, right?". He hastily responded "no" and cut the call. I did not see the point in being angry. In fact, I should have been the one to be angry at him. He could have at least called and told me that the bus was canceled. Come on! Time wasted and to top that the hope I was hanging on to was shattered again. My roommates started walking back home. I did not even feel like calling it home anymore. I felt betrayed, cheated, and disappointed yet again. It was about 9 AM, we were in our apartment when I saw the news about discrimination against anyone of color. I personally hadn't felt it yet but there were multiple shreds of evidence of how people of color were being pushed behind from the border, they were not allowed to board the trains, and they were being pushed back and mistreated. Men were being beaten up, while some officials reportedly pulled on the hair of the women. It was easier for Ukrainian citizens to cross.

There was no bunker in our building so we decided to go to hostel no. 2 as they have a basement there. The continuous air-raid sirens were not for practice this time. They were real. We said our last goodbyes to this apartment. There were many memories there, some happy, some frustrating, and others sad. My roommate called their friends in the hostel, asking if they can stay there too. Getting a positive response, we packed our things (which were already packed) and locked the place. I thought to myself "is this goodbye forever?" But that was the least of my concerns. The air raid sirens were blaring loud. We reached the hostel within 20 minutes and straight went to the basement as the whole hostel was bunkered down. The fear was real. The uncertainty, on the other hand, of whether we will live or die was high. The air raid sirens kept going for about an hour. They had become more frequent since yesterday. Did that mean Lviv was in trouble or was there a bomb thrown toward Lviv? We came out of our hiding. Our friends in the hostel gave us some snacks they had left. They were also from Hyderabad and spoke the language as I did. It was eternally kind of them to offer us food since nobody knows when they will cross the border and groceries were limited. We discussed our escape plans at length but in the end, the conclusion was that if we are not with the embassy, they won't allow us, and we might be manhandled.

Social media was high in the Russia-Ukraine war. But India decided to badmouth the students studying in a different country saying "they deserve to die" or "why are they blaming the government now" or "after all they are those "mandbudhi" MBBS aspirants". Mandbudhi is a Hindi word that means a mad person. There were even worse comments on several YouTube videos and Twitter. I did not even know what to say or how to react to all this.

We did not know that Putin was going to launch a full-scale invasion. Even the Ukrainian government thought it was all a gimmick. Yes, there were some intelligence reports but we all thought that it will be limited to the eastern (DONBAS) region just like in 2013-2014. The response, however, was quite tragic. The hatred was so strong that they are ready to write such things openly. The Indian embassy issued advisories that non-essential people may go back to India and the flights that were "especially" arranged were priced around 800-1000USD for one person.

Yes, I am a mad person to leave my family and friends to go to a country that is completely unknown to me.

Yes, I am crazy because I cannot afford to pay thousands of dollars for private medical school.

Yes, I am insane because I want to become a doctor.

I am not great at showing emotions. I was infuriated within and wanted to personally call this person and shout at him. But would that change anything? I don't think so. People are jealous and resentful. We were speaking about these things when Ashok anna called wanting to know what happened. This 2nd disappointment was rather a smaller one, I guess. It is like I am used to disappointments now. I said, "No, they are not allowing any Indians across the border unless you are with the Indian embassy". I also added, "I will wait for the embassy". He said "Ok". We were a total of 6-7 people in hostel no. 2 and were trying to come up with a plan. The embassy suggested for the students in the western region wait as they first wanted the evacuate the students studying in the eastern parts of Ukraine. One of them suggested that we should travel to Uzzhorod and cross the Romanian border because the Indian embassy got 400 students across from there. At least, if the officials see us, they would take us with them. It was a long shot but traveling across Ukraine can be dangerous, not-to-mention, with which vehicle are we going to travel. Everyone is trying to cash in the desperateness. The taxi drivers are asking 500USD. The people arranging the bus are asking for 750USD. We had now the following options in front of us.

Waiting for the embassy as the current advisory read those students who are not from L'viv will be transported across Shehyni-Polish border.

Traveling to Uzzhorod and TRYING to cross the Romanian border by bus which asked 750 USD per person.

Traveling by taxi by paying 500 USD to the Polish border again to TRY ourselves.

Nobody knew which one was the best one or rather the one that would help them to just cross the border.

Meanwhile, they decided to cook some food as they had a huge stash of vegetables, rice, flour, and snacks. Nobody has eaten since morning. Between the air-raid sirens and I contacted my parents and gave them the bad news which made the situation worse in India. My sister and my brother-in-law also called and we had a long conversation. What I gathered from my parents was also the same thing, that it is better to wait for the embassy. Traveling was not safe at this point. Speaking helps but it was up to me to make the final decision because I am here and only, I can assess and understand the gravity of the situation. For today, the 7 of us decided to wait it out since it was already too late to even go anywhere. The waiting period at the Polish border is about 24-48 hours. The Iranian senior was denied entry to the Hungarian border and so he decided to come to L'viv and try to cross the Polish border. He did not get any sleep for the last two nights. They were sleeping inside the car for a few hours. Thankfully, the petrol stations had enough fuel for the car so that they could switch on the heat and sleep. According to him, last night, they slept in the cold. That is brutal. The war had become truly ruthless to us (the people who wanted to have a normal life). He had reached the Polish border and was now waiting. He was 15 km away from the border. It is going to be super disappointing if he is not allowed after waiting for about 48 hours. According to the UN, there were reports of 400,000 people crossing the border and thousands more displaced from their homes and are on the move. I guess I am one of them.

Russian forces had attacked the Chernobyl power plant. The power plant has remained closed for years. What did Russia want from Chernobyl? Also, they entered Kyiv and were roaming with tanks on the streets. You don't want to witness tanks and weapons and artillery on the streets. I honestly thought humanity was making progress and that we are moving toward a more tolerable and open-minded society. Alas, that was not the case. One man had the power to disrupt my life, and career in just a few minutes. That is why we have democracy and we need democracy.

Here I was thinking the pandemic of COVID-19 or global warming would be the last of my problems in this century. I laughed at that within. Russia and Ukraine wanted to have peace talks. That was a sign of something good. It means there could be a ceasefire. Russia wanted Ukraine to surrender while Ukraine demanded a ceasefire before the meeting at the border of Belarus. None of that happened. Earlier the meeting was supposed to be held in Belarus but President Zelensky said that since Belarus was being used as a territory to fire at us, we are not going inside the country. Finally, after hours of anticipation, the meeting was held at the border of Belarus. Meanwhile, the world leaders of the US and EU had ordered harsh economic sanctions on Russia which led to increased frustration in Kremlin. As we all guessed, there was no ceasefire. In fact, even during the peace talks, Russia continued its bombarding. Yes, so Russia had no plans of stopping the attacks or peace. That made things even harder for me. The little hope left in my heart had faded away and a cold wave of sadness and frustration appeared.

Thankfully, my face never really shows what I was feeling since I don't like to talk too much. The more expressions your face show, the more questions people ask. I was in no mood to answer anyone. But I did feel a lot of fear and uncertainty. My chain of thoughts was broken by the amazing smell of Indian food. It has been a while since I cooked or ate something Indian. They had some rice and dal along with mango pickle. The sheer taste of the spicy pickle brought back the happy memories of when I was at home in India or the happy times with my friends in Ukraine. This meal might be the last one if the next bomb falls here. There have been several reports of bombs on residential areas and buildings. I tried very hard not to think pessimistically but the situation did not leave me with a choice. It was already 4 PM since all that had happened. After having the delicious food, I was just looking into my phone as the others were speaking or crying or laughing. I guess, everyone had their way of coping with this situation. Apart from our misery, there was an added tension in our homes where every parent was calling every 1 or 2 hours to check on us. Sometimes you would hear them crying and other times you would hear them shouting. One of my friend's mothers thought this was the best time to say "I told you there was going to be war. Why don't you listen to me? You are so irresponsible. Have I raised you to be like this? Now, look at yourself! You are stuck. What will my friends and society think of me?" Since it was the same language and I could understand everything but I wished I wouldn't have. I couldn't believe my ears. I understand that they are going through a tough time but your child is in the situation. Shouting or saying such negative things will not help anyone. He excused himself and went outside the room and listen to some more of that negative reinforcement.

Suddenly I woke up to my phone ringing. I must have drifted off while looking at the latest news. My roommate was like "your phone has been ringing nonstop. This is the 5th time". I asked him "Is there a new bomb in

L'viv or something"? He said, "No. but Putin has decided to send a message by saying that he is ready to launch Nuclear weapons". I picked up the phone and the moment my mother heard my voice, she started crying. I felt helpless and wanted to hug her. I said "Mom, please don't cry. If you keep crying, where will I get the strength." She said "No, my dear son. You are the strongest and bravest of all and I just want to see you again live and well. I just heard from your father that some of your friends were beaten up at the border and that they are not letting them board the train". I left a huge sigh and said "Yes ma. It is unfortunate but such cases of racism are common here. That is why I decided to go with the embassy". She replied agreeing "yes yes, that is the right decision son. When will the embassy arrange transportation for you?" In my mind, I thought I wish I knew but lied to her again saying "Tonight they will take the other kids from the eastern part, and tomorrow they will take the kids from the western part because East is in much higher danger. There are more cases of bombarding." I think she was happy because there was a plan, hope, and a small ray of sunshine at the end of the tunnel (whatever you want to call it). For me, it was bland lies and truly I had no plans. All we were doing was "waiting it out". I shivered at that thought and told my mother that I had to go and do something like some kind of online paperwork for the embassy. My mother calmingly said, "ok son. Be careful. Don't go out alone". I cut the call after agreeing to all the things and added that I am not doing any of those. Also, I said that I will call her once I get to know something from the embassy. The Indian embassy had crossed about 400 students across the Romanian border as opposed to over 20,000 students still left in the destruction caused by Russian bombs and tanks.

The embassy should have launched a full-scale evacuation 3 days ago when they said "if you want, you may leave "and not put flights worth 800USD. But then nobody imagined this would be the case. I guess the "diplomatic relations" are not as close between India and Russia as the world thinks.

The war brought an unusual thing to our lives: people who never spoke to us started messaging and calling asking about our well-being. Well, here is something you need to know about Indian relatives, they are usually jealous, and pass sarcastic comments to whatever you have to say. There might be some who are genuinely interested in your well-being but they are few. Most of them will never help you unless they have a hidden agenda. If they do, the whole world must know. I decided to not engage with such people right now. I know the first thing they would say "why did you go so far to study medicine? You should have done something here." It is somehow justifiable if it is their son or daughter. I had a lot on my plate. I spoke to the people I care about like my parents, my grandparents, my sister and her husband, a few seniors in India, my close friends in India, and of course my girlfriend. I even wanted her to come to Ukraine this year so that I can show her around and spend some quality time together. She has never been to a different country. She has even been to very few places in India. I intended to show her the beautiful world I have seen and more. But that would never happen. I don't know what would happen to Ukraine after the war ends and if the war ends at all. The strong Ukrainian resistance has made it difficult for the Russian troops to do what they wanted to do overnight. However, Putin has enough force to achieve what he wants. I was out of the room as I spoke to one person after another. Finally, when all those calls finished, I went back to the room and saw my friends packing. One of them said "come on, get ready. I just got a call that a group of Indians has crossed the Hungarian border from Uzzhorod. We will also try the same." I replied, "that is great. They are with the embassy? Will the embassy wait for us? What about...". "I don't know all those details Kumar. Right now, we are leaving. Can you call that taxi guy?" I was like "Guys, we might not be able to cross. People of color are being mistreated. I don't want to go this far just to come back again. Plus it is late and you know the attacks are happening at night". One of my roommates agreed with me adding "omg, I didn't even think about those attacks. It has been so quiet in here. I think we should start in the morning. Like early morning 4 AM or 5 AM". The guy who started the Uzzhorod conversation said, "don't you guys want to leave the country? Like I don't understand what is happening here. See my friend just crossed the border". To that, I replied, "See, I understand your frustration but you need some more details. Going all the way to Uzzhorod is not a child's play". Another girl added, "Look, guys, foreigners are being beaten up on the streets. They can even kill us and no one will give a shit". My roommate said, "exactly and that is exactly why we need a concrete plan". That guy finally agreed as everyone tried to convince him saying "ok fine. It is 10 PM already. Just start looking for a taxi and let us leave at 6 AM. The plan is simple. We will reach the border by around 11 AM tomorrow and join the line to cross the border. Once they see that we have Indian passports, they will let us pass. That is what my friend said "

I was on taxi duty, just because our landlord was very nice to me and gave us the contact of a relative of hers. I called him and started explaining the situation. He understood English. Thank goodness. He replied saying "ok but it will be 500$". I was in shock "for one person!!". He said, "well if you are alone. It is for the whole ride for one car". I tried to hold my shock and disbelief and said "well, we are 7 people. That means we need 2 cars, right?" He said, "yes! That will be 1000$". I cut the call after saying that I need to talk to my other friends and call him back. I went up to my friends and told them the situation. It was 2 AM and nobody looked like they wanted to sleep. I said "guys, we need 1000$ for 2 cars for the whole ride. He will leave us a few kilometers before the border as usual. We might have to walk about 5-6 kilometers." There were 4 boys and 3 girls on our group in the hostel. One of the girls started crying and as I guessed the reason was she did not have enough money. She was one of those girls who go to clubs and pubs and wears expensive dresses. So, I guess, that is where all her money went. But drama aside, it was a huge sum of money to be gathered all at once with the banks on the brink of failure. I had 400USD because of the refund from my flight. She was not the only one, a few others were also falling short of money. Even for the people who included the money, it was not adding up to 1000USD. We were 200USD short. I tried calling the taxi driver but he did not pick up. Maybe he was driving or sleeping. It was 3 AM after all. I told them that he is not picking, and I will try again in the morning. I was mentally exhausted. This time I did not even need my phone to fall asleep.

CHAPTER FIVE

24 HOURS

28/02/2022 Sunday

I was walking through the ruins of Kyiv. Kids were sitting and crying. Bodies piled up everywhere. "KYIV!!! WHY THE HELL AM I IN KYIV" I shouted and woke up completely drenched in sweat. OK, that was a dream. We have studied in Neurology that your subconscious dictates the dreams most of the time. Therefore, my dreams reflected the deep-seated fear I have of what the war can and will bring - eternal destruction. It was way past the time we were supposed to leave. I saw everyone was sleeping and it was 10 AM. I tried to wake my roommate up but he was deep in sleep. I thought about whether the plan was canceled or if there was any change of plans. What will we do now? Where will we go?

My daily morning routine of checking Instagram has changed to checking the Indian embassy website if they released a new advisory to evacuate us (students of Lviv). Several thousand students from the Eastern parts of Ukraine had crossed the border on Saturday and were now on their way to India. I wish I was one of them. Definitely, I understand that they were under grave danger in Kyiv and Kharkiv and other eastern states but who can vouch that Putin's next target will not be Lviv? Nobody! He is deranged and he will do whatever it takes. There was nothing from the embassy yet again. They have been eerily quiet about the students from Lviv and the neighboring cities. Will we ever be able to cross over to the safer side? Is this going to be my life? Am I going to die in this country?

The thoughts were negative but legitimate. I was not a Ukrainian citizen or a white person and that had made things super difficult. Even during this war-time people find a way to discriminate. I wasn't surprised. I have been attacked before when I was in my first year. 4 Ukrainian guys came and started hitting me and my senior as we stopped our car after an accident. I do not remember what happened but my senior told me that I went into a seizure. I am not good at confronting or fighting. I like to live my life in peace. I did everything by the book, filing a police report, waiting, but those bastards were never caught. So yeah, I had my unfair share of racism and discrimination. And now, they were doing it in the open without any remorse or regret. I did not start a fight with anyone. I did not do anything wrong to any Ukrainian but I had felt the hit much harder than anyone else.

This time, it was different. Even if they were doing discrimination or hitting us, I just wanted to cross the border. I was ready to be discriminated against just for the sake of crossing the border. It was 12 PM and my stomach was churning with hunger. My brain on the other hand forgot to release the hunger hormone because I wasn't feeling it one bit. Imagine you wake up; you have a whole day planned in front of you. Get ready. Go to school. Study. Attend lectures. Come back and sleep or go out to the center depending on the weather. Well, now it had turned to wake up and think of a way to leave this country. In addition to that, I was worried about my future studies and completion of the degree. My parents had spent a lot of money and not to forget the time invested into this. Nothing can replace the 5 years I spent here.

I went up to the fridge and saw there were eggs. I took one egg and some bread and went to the kitchen. I made a toast and ate it. Water scarcity was evident. We were 7 people and just had one can of water (5 liters). I had some water in my bottle and took a few drops to quench the long-standing thirst of 14-15 hours. I thought we might have to start drinking tap water. I will cross that bridge when we come to it. Do I need to cross that bridge? Don't I deserve peace??

Finally, all my friends started waking up in a panic. Just like me, they had no idea what to do and how to continue. That Uzzhorod plan was on hold because if we start now, we would reach by about 4 PM and then walking an hour or two more, it might get dark, and then how will we get back or where will we stay? Too many questions but no answers. Also, not to forget that the taxi driver never called back or showed up. They wanted to go to the grocery store. Since there were no sirens, three of them went out. I asked "So what is the plan? Are we waiting or crossing?" one of the guys who likes to be the boss said "Well another group just passed the Hungarian border. If you didn't oppose, we would have crossed by now" I responded calmly

"Look. This is not helping anyone. I never opposed I just...." He again cut me in the middle "ah ah ah. You see. Now you are saying you did not oppose. Of course, you will change sides bro." I just left the room. I did not have the energy to argue with mindless morons.

As I was sitting on the windowsill in the corridor, I saw a message pop up. She was a friend from Ivano. I thought it is going to be another "How are you? How is everything?" because she was in India. Since I wasn't doing anything better, I looked at the message

"Hey! So, we are at the Polish border, and looks like they are letting them pass without any problems."

"The Indian government has pressurized them to let anyone with an Indian passport pass".

I replied saying

"You are not in India?"

She wrote

"No. I booked a ticket but you know the war and all. It got canceled."

Just hurry up and join"

I was beyond thrilled and wrote

"Ok. That is great. Can you please send me the address or share the location?"

She wrote

"Sure! See you on the other side ?"

She sent a picture of where she was and shared her location through WhatsApp. Thank goodness, the internet was still working as usual.

I hurried back inside and told them about what I received. I even showed them the pictures sent by her. She sent a picture of her passport with a stamp that she crossed the border to Poland. This was all great news. According to her, several groups have passed but it might take 5-6 hours. I called my Iranian senior who was still 5 km away from the border. He said "we are about to cross. Everything is fine here. What about you?" I said "Ok. Nice. We will also cross the polish border" He replied, "are you sure?" I said "yes, many Indians are crossing the border. They are just looking at our passports and letting us cross." He said "ok. That is great. Keep me posted". It was already 3 PM so we should hurry and leave for the border. There were 4 motorways to cross the border with Poland, Rava Rus'ka, Shehyni, Krakovets, and Khyriv. Rava rus'ka and Shehyni had a waiting line for about 20 km for those borders. I thought that our best bet would be Krakovets but that wasn't the case. My friend sent us a location of another border called Budomezh-Hrushiv. There was a narrow street completely covered by forest on both sides. That is what the Google map showed.

Thankfully, there was no resistance to my idea because I showed them the proof. We booked 2 taxis who demanded 1000USD. The taxi services were back to normal. It was also a way to earn hard cash for the drivers right now. We said I am sorry but we just have 800USD cash. The cab driver agreed. I just wanted to leave this warzone.

By the time, we got ready and left, it was already 6 PM. Yes, even when we are in a crisis, people had to wear make-up, do their hair, and take an hour. As we made our way to the border, I was reminded of the time, I came back disappointed. Yes, there were like 90% chances that I come back but..... that tiny "but" kept me alive and hopeful. Half of us were already dead inside. The news updates were not particularly positive but there was one news that was beyond terrible. One Indian guy died in Kharkiv when he went to buy some groceries. That was the first death of color in Ukraine. I cannot imagine what his parents are going through right now. This made me even more determined to cross the border. I called my parents and a few friends in India telling them about our plan to cross the border over to Poland. I also told them how Indians are being allowed easily since they have been pressurized by the Indian government. This pressure was honestly the thing required right now.

The scenes at the border were heart-breaking. The news was constantly flashing as we were going towards the border in the taxi. There were still people crying and distressed. Women and children leave their husbands, fathers, and brothers to fight. Several women volunteered to fight. Ukraine's military received a total of 18,000 volunteers who were ready to fight for their country. Now that is what I call Patriotism. The death of the Indian kid had brought another set of retweets and Insta stories. While some showed sympathy, others continued to ridicule him for studying outside India.

BORDERLINE PSYCHOTIC MORONS!!

I did not want to think more about this and wanted to look at the brighter side. As I was searching for one, I saw on the news that a missile landed in L'viv. I couldn't hear or see anything but that was bad news. Lviv was a haven and now there was destruction and chaos. Nobody knew if died there were deaths or how many were injured. Lviv was hope for millions of Ukrainians and other people of color. But now it wasn't safe either. It took us about 2 hours to reach the border. The congestion on the roads hadn't been relieved at all. In fact, it is increasing by the hour, especially in L'viv.

Around 8:15 PM, we got down from the taxi and walked around an hour more. The border was relatively empty. I saw a group of African students, standing in groups near the border. I did not know anyone personally but people of color not standing in line was bad news. The only reason I could think about was that they are not letting foreigners cross the border. I called the girl who texted. She informed me that she had already crossed the border a few hours ago and now they are in Poland and were provided with food, water, and accommodation. I told her that I am also at the border and have joined the line. There was another group of Indians ahead of us, followed by some Ukrainians. Approximately there were 50-60 people before us. We silently joined the line and patiently waited for our chance. I texted my senior and my girlfriend in India that I was at the border. I had called my parents before leaving because it was already midnight in India. My heart skipped a beat in happiness when I saw the other group of Indians pass smoothly without any hassle or fights. After about 1 hour, our group reached the border. To my surprise, they simply took all our 7 passports, saw that we were Indian citizens, put stamps inside our passports, and let us go.

That was it. It was about 3 AM. People say it was the time for ghosts and spirits to come out. But that day 3 AM was the time of freedom. The check post at the Polish side did not stop us either. They showed us the way to a tent where we could get a cup of tea, and some warmth. The winter did not show mercy at all. There was a cruel cold wind blowing throughout this time but the adrenaline rush of finally crossing the border had decreased the cold by half.

In the morning (after about 3 hours), all the Indians were gathered near the check post and were asked to board a bus that would take us to our accommodation set up by the Indian government. The bus was accompanied by Polish police convoys in the front and behind the bus and it did not stop at any signal just like diplomats. I always wondered how it felt to go like a VIP. Well, thanks to Operation Ganga, I have finally lived it. The Polish roads were beyond whatever I had imagined. They were bigger, cleaner, and had no potholes. Some of my seniors who have been to European countries have told me that Ukraine is nothing like Europe and now I can finally say that whatever they have said, it is all true. We were being taken to the nearest city called Rzeszow from where we will be taking our flights to India. Within 2 hours, we reached the city. I slept through the whole bus journey compensating for the lost sleep over the past

96 hours. The hotel we were staying at was a 4-start hotel. Surprisingly, the Indian government had really outdone itself this time or maybe they did this even before, I don't know. Once I reached my room, I immediately hit the showers. Frankly speaking, I don't remember the last time, I had a nice warm shower in L'viv. My friends wanted to go and explore, I told them to continue without me, I had to make a few calls. I posted on Snapchat and WhatsApp my location once I crossed the border. That eased the tension among many people in India including my girlfriend. I called my mother after the shower:

"Mother, I am in Poland. Everything is fine."

My mother did not even try to hold her tears back. I think they were tears of happiness and continued

"Oh, my dear child. I have prayed day and night for you. Have you eaten something? Did you get some sleep? Were you beaten up at the border?"

I replied

"Mother mother. This is a happy time. Please don't cry. Yes, I ate food. Some people at the Polish border gave some warm food and tea. We also got water. I slept for some time but then had to take a bus to this hotel and no, nobody touched me and any of us. The Indian government has done a good job. Mother, have you found any sleep yet?"

I knew that she would never talk about the fact she also couldn't sleep just like me and could not push the food down her throat without shedding any tears.

She replied

"I will sleep, son. Now I will sleep. My son is safe and I will see him soon. When are you coming to India?"

I said "I think, we have a flight for tomorrow afternoon so I will be in Delhi by 6 PM today. I will check in with the Indian embassy and let you know for sure. But I am just so happy I am finally free, Mother"

We went on to talk about several other things like the garden in India and father's business. She added sadly, "I got really bad news from her about one Indian guy getting killed in Kharkiv". My mother wanted to know if he was a friend of mine. I checked some of the tweets and saw about that guy. I did not know him personally. I told my mother that he was not a friend of mine. I don't think I cannot imagine the grief, his friends, and his family is going through right now. He went shopping for groceries and the building was hit by a missile. What I gathered from the news was that he was dead immediately.

I spoke with my father and sister for a while afterward. I also made sure I texted my girlfriend. When she is at the university, she doesn't pick up the call. Today when i texted her, i saw her call. It must have been 10 AM in India. I was like how is she calling at this time. I picked up the call and said "aren't you at the university?"

She replied, "I am but I left the class. That stupid professor saw the phone. Before he could say it, I took my bag and left the class. I don't care about anything right now. Are you okay?"

I said, "yes, I am absolutely fine. Thanks for your prayers I guess. We crossed the border within minutes. Can you imagine! The Indian government made sure all Indian passport holders pass the border without a problem. You might receive a remark from your professor na. Go back to your class!"

She happily said, "who cares about his remarks. But yes, exams are nearby, I will tell him that I had a period emergency and get back in class. LOL. I am so happy to see you again Chinnu. That is what my girlfriend called me.

Now I can understand what our freedom fighters must have felt like, what the people of India felt when the Britishers retreated. Of course, it was not the same fight but the feeling of freedom inside me was the same.

Many Indians, Africans, Egyptians, and Ukrainians were still stuck inside the country. Some weren't even trying to flee because they believed that everything will be fine. I hope that happens but given the circumstances, chances are slim.

I was finally free.

CHAPTER SIX

LAST THOUGHTS

Telling a story from far is easy. I cannot possibly understand what the people of Ukraine and the foreign students studying in Ukraine went through. My writing process included a lot of my imagination, apart from what the students living in Ukraine told me. The whole point of writing this story was to put some spotlight over the students from other countries who were denied exit at the borders, who were mistreated, and those who lost their lives. I was lucky to be able to escape the brutal war and terrorism that Russia has impaled over Ukraine. It was a place where I learned the meaning of freedom, and also I understood that I am not a 16-year-old girl anymore. As I was going through my studies, I also had to take care of a ton of paperwork, do the dishes, clean the place and make sure I was succeeding in life. It wasn't easy, but it is one that has taught me the meaning of life. It makes my heart quiver when I think about the destruction in the beautiful cities of Ukraine and people dying. When I go through the pictures flooding through social media, I see myself walking over the same streets. The only difference is that when I am walking, there is peace and serenity in it, while the pictures have blood of innocent people all over the streets. As a doctor, I can only imagine the horror the healthcare personnel have to deal with day in and out. Is this the world you imagined yourself to be in? I honestly did not see a war coming through. When people talked about "World War 3", I always puffed it away, like removing the smoke from in front of you. There are many students who are still in Ukraine because the Indian Government (in particular the National Medical Council of India) decided that this is the best time to release the following statement:

"Central Government has told the Supreme Court that Ukraine returned medical students cannot be admitted in Indian universities as National Medical Commission Act doesn't allow it. The Centre also stated that students went to foreign countries due to two reasons - poor merit in NEET and affordability"

September 15, 2022, NDTV

Many careers have been destroyed. Many lives ruined. And currently, as I am writing, several students are risking their lives living in Ukraine to complete their education. As you and I are waking up to the sound of alarm or the birds in certain places, those students and people of Ukraine are probably lying through the blaring sounds of sirens and fear of bombs. I have no more words.

#StopThe War

Now A Few Accounts From The Students Who Were And Are Still In Ukraine.

1. Dickson Ojama (A Nigerian guy from Kyiv)

"During the war, the terrifying blast, and the confusion caused by the bomb, crippled my ability to make a sound decisions. Also, I learned that logistics and cash are very important things"

2. Moses Tse Gboga (A Nigerian guy from Odessa)

"I have not been in a position to directly face hostility, but I have seen many familiar persons experience racist treatment while trying to leave Ukraine during the war. I have been staying at home since the day the war started."

3. Mode Yogananda (Ivano Frankivska)

"I faced only one struggle, standing and waiting at the border for more than 12 hours."

4. Revanth Raj (An Indian from Ivano Frankivska)

"I didn't believe any rumors about the war. I thought it will not happen but once there was an airstrike on Feb 24 I was in a shock, though I wasn't scared much. It was a new experience, exhausting and tiring once in a lifetime will never forget it."

5. Himansh Kumar P. (An Indian from Ivano Frankivska)

"I came back to India about a week before the bombarding started. I feel very bad for what's going on in Ukraine, so many families lost their members, and they are on the roads in some towns. Not only that, but I don't know how it feels to leave their loved once in the war and leave your country and go to another one. Most of the foreign students has being affected because of the war, mainly the final year students' education got interrupted. They were mentally prepared for their exams and had plans for their careers and now because of this war everything got disrupted. If there are any issues between any countries, the governments have to settle it diplomatically."

6. Anonymous (An Indian from Kharkiv)

"The people were so brave in Ukraine. They didn't fear for the one of the most powerful armies in the world. I have seen true patriotism in the people. During the war crisis, everyone were helping each other."

7. Archana Rajput (An Indian from Lviv)

"Ukraine is the such a wonderful place with a great culture and I loved the environment, it's so peaceful. Unfortunately, the war created chaos and fear."

Printed by Libri Plureos GmbH in Hamburg,
Germany